†**Bishop Edward M. Grosz, D.D.**

BOOKS & MEDIA

Boston

Cover and title page photo: Sr. M. Emmanuel Alves, FSP

Stations of the Cross art: Sisters of the Holy Cross

ISBN 0-8198-8299-2

All rights reserved. No part of this book may be reproduced or transmitted in any form or by any means, electronic or mechanical, including photocopying, recording or by any information storage and retrieval system, without permission in writing from the publisher.

Copyright © 1999, Daughters of St. Paul

Printed and published in the U.S.A. by Pauline Books & Media, 50 Saint Pauls Avenue, Boston MA 02130-3491.

www.pauline.org

Pauline Books & Media is the publishing house of the Daughters of St. Paul, an international congregation of women religious serving the Church with the communications media.

3 4 5 6 7 8 9   08 07 06 05 04 03

Leader	In the name of the Father, and of the Son, and of the Holy Spirit. ***(Stand)***
All	Amen.

INTRODUCTION

All	Lord Jesus, I am about to walk with you the way of the cross which you accepted in obedience to the will of your Father. As I reflect upon each of these stations, recalling what you experienced in your passion and death, may the grace of your Holy Spirit touch my mind and heart, as I grow in my desire to do your Father's will day by day, just as you did. With our Blessed Lady, your sorrowful Mother, and all the holy ones through the centuries, I want to do my best to mirror in my daily life the teachings of your Gospel message, as I continue to witness to you, the Way, the Truth, and the Life.
Leader	Lord Jesus crucified, Son of the living God,
All	Have mercy on me a sinner. ***(Stand)***
	Hymn (see options on page 35 ff.)

The First Station | JESUS IS CONDEMNED TO DEATH

Leader	We adore you, O Christ, and we praise you. *(Kneel)*
All	For by your holy cross you have redeemed the world. *(Stand)*
Leader	Lord Jesus, in your appearance before Pontius Pilate you suffered a great mockery of justice—although innocent, you were condemned. Yet you accepted it for love of us. *(Kneel)*
All	Beloved Master Jesus, at times I am the object of injustice when I am falsely accused. I also see around me signs of injustice when others are made to suffer. As I face such moments in life, stand by my side to affirm me, to guide me, and to strengthen me to respond as you would. As I stand before others as a witness to the truth—your truth and your Gospel message—help me to act in the way you taught.
Leader	Lord Jesus crucified,
All	Have mercy on me a sinner. *(Stand)*
	Hymn

The Second Station | JESUS ACCEPTS HIS CROSS

Leader	We adore you, O Christ, and we praise you. ***(Kneel)***
All	For by your holy cross you have redeemed the world. ***(Stand)***
Leader	Lord Jesus, you willingly accepted the burden of the cross in an act of total abandonment to the Father. This is the obedience you ask of those who follow you. ***(Kneel)***
All	Brother Jesus, you remind us in your Gospel, "If any want to become my followers, let them deny themselves and take up their cross daily and follow me" (Lk 9:23).
	Lord Jesus, give me the strength and the grace to accept the cross that comes to me in the challenges of daily living. Help me to act courageously in facing the difficulties that enter my life. May I remember your words "Come to me, all you that are weary and are carrying heavy burdens, and I will give you rest" (Mt. 11:28).
Leader	Lord Jesus crucified,
All	Have mercy on me a sinner. ***(Stand)***
	Hymn

The Third Station | JESUS FALLS THE FIRST TIME

Leader	We adore you, O Christ, and we praise you. ***(Kneel)***
All	For by your holy cross you have redeemed the world. ***(Stand)***
Leader	Brother Jesus, everything you have suffered has drained you of strength. Your exhaustion and weakness caused you to fall beneath the cross for the first time. Yet, you stood up again and bore that cross on the road to Calvary. ***(Kneel)***
All	Dear Jesus, when my cross weighs me down and I fall, give me the courage and strength to stand up again and continue my journey through life. When so many daily difficulties burden me, grant me your gift of peace, courage, and strength to face each new challenge in life.
Leader	Lord Jesus crucified,
All	Have mercy on me a sinner. ***(Stand)***
	Hymn

The Fourth Station | JESUS MEETS HIS SORROWFUL MOTHER

Leader	We adore you, O Christ, and we praise you. ***(Kneel)***
All	For by your holy cross you have redeemed the world. ***(Stand)***
Leader	What thoughts and feelings must have raced through your Mother's mind and heart, as she saw you treated with such contempt! Yes, Lord Jesus, her heart was heavy with the pain of seeing her Son treated in such a cruel manner. How much her heart went out to you! All she could do was to be at your side along that painful way of the cross. ***(Kneel)***
All	Lord Jesus, as I journey through life, I am conscious of the presence of the woman you gave to us to be our Mother, your holy Mother Mary, Mother of the Church. May she, our sorrowful Mother, continue to be at my side to comfort me as I face the hardships, worries and pains of daily living. May she lead me ever closer to you, as she walks with me in life to guide me along the way of discipleship. Bless all mothers, Lord Jesus, for all of the pain and sorrow they have borne for their children. May Mary ever be their source of consolation and hope.
Leader	Lord Jesus crucified,
All	Have mercy on me a sinner. ***(Stand)*** *Hymn*

The Fifth Station | SIMON OF CYRENE HELPS JESUS CARRY THE CROSS

Leader	We adore you, O Christ, and we praise you. ***(Kneel)***
All	For by your holy cross you have redeemed the world. ***(Stand)***
Leader	No doubt, Lord Jesus, you felt a sense of relief when the soldiers brought forth Simon of Cyrene to help you bear the heavy weight of your cross. Then it became less of a burden to you. ***(Kneel)***
All	Lord Jesus, I thank you for the people you send into my life to help me bear the burdens of daily living. When sorrow, pain and trouble enter my life, there always seems to be that special person who comes to my side to assist me. Lord Jesus, bless all of those who have assisted me in times of need. Lord Jesus, help me also to look for opportunities to help others bear their burdens, as I face the challenge to be your faithful and loving witness and disciple in today's world.
Leader	Lord Jesus crucified,
All	Have mercy on me a sinner. ***(Stand)*** *Hymn*

The Sixth Station: VERONICA WIPES THE FACE OF JESUS

Leader	We adore you, O Christ, and we praise you. *(Kneel)*
All	For by your holy cross you have redeemed the world. *(Stand)*
Leader	Lord Jesus, Veronica stepped forward from the crowd to be with you as you faced your time of trial and suffering. As she wiped the blood and sweat from your face, how relieved you must have felt, especially because you saw in her face an expression of your Gospel, calling others to tenderness, compassion and concern. *(Kneel)*
All	Lord of Lords, help me to be like Veronica. Help me to look for opportunities to show the compassion, concern and love you ask of your faithful witnesses and disciples. Lord Jesus, bless all of those Veronicas in my life, who have helped me or who have taken time to share with me words of affirmation, support, or encouragement. Bless them and help me to see your face in those who suffer.
Leader	Lord Jesus crucified,
All	Have mercy on me a sinner. *(Stand)*
	Hymn

The Seventh Station | JESUS FALLS THE SECOND TIME

Leader	We adore you, O Christ, and we praise you. *(Kneel)*
All	For by your holy cross you have redeemed the world. *(Stand)*
Leader	Weakened from loss of blood and the strain of bearing the cross, you fell a second time, Lord Jesus. Yet, you struggled to get up again to continue your journey to Calvary. *(Kneel)*
All	Brother Jesus, as I face whatever humiliation and distress life brings, give me the courage and strength to rise above them. Lord Jesus, help me also to support others and help them as they face suffering in their lives.
Leader	Lord Jesus crucified,
All	Have mercy on me a sinner. *(Stand)*
	Hymn

The Eighth Station: JESUS SPEAKS TO THE WOMEN

Leader	We adore you, O Christ, and we praise you. ***(Kneel)***
All	For by your holy cross you have redeemed the world. ***(Stand)***
Leader	What a great comfort these women must have been for you, Lord Jesus! They felt compassion for you when they saw you in pain under the weight of the cross. How thoughtful they were! How pleased you must have been to see them and accept their expression of understanding, love and concern. ***(Kneel)***
All	I thank you, Lord Jesus, for all those women in my life who have given me strength and support. I thank you for my mother, who gave me the gift of life and has supported me along the journey of life. I thank you for all the women who have been a source of great consolation, affirmation and moral support—doctors, religious, teachers, aunts, grandmothers, sisters, married women, single women. Bless each one of them, living and deceased. Help me to appreciate the beautiful gift of womanhood as manifested in the faith-filled and loving example of your holy Mother, Mary.
Leader	Lord Jesus crucified,
All	Have mercy on me a sinner. ***(Stand)***
	Hymn

The Ninth Station | JESUS FALLS THE THIRD TIME

Leader	We adore you, O Christ, and we praise you. ***(Kneel)***
All	For by your holy cross you have redeemed the world. ***(Stand)***
Leader	A third time you fell under the weight of the cross, Lord Jesus. Many along the road must have wondered if you would be able to finish that pain-filled journey to Calvary. Yet, as they watched, you struggled to get up again and, assisted by Simon of Cyrene, continued on your way. ***(Kneel)***
All	Sometimes, Lord Jesus, when I fall under the weight of life's misfortunes, others may wonder if I will ever get up again. I may face a critical illness; I may face a serious challenge to my self-esteem or sense of integrity. Yes, Lord Jesus, I too may wonder how I will get up again and face the demands of daily living. But in spite of all of this, I know that you will be with me through your grace and example to help me get up again and continue to live life to its fullest.
	Lord Jesus, be my strength, my hope, and my protection.
Leader	Lord Jesus crucified,
All	Have mercy on me a sinner. ***(Stand)***
	Hymn

The Tenth Station | JESUS IS STRIPPED OF HIS GARMENTS

Leader	We adore you, O Christ, and we praise you. *(Kneel)*
All	For by your holy cross you have redeemed the world. *(Stand)*
Leader	The soldiers wanted to disgrace you because they stripped you of your garments in public. They wanted to make a mockery of you, someone stripped of his dignity!

How humiliated you must have felt, as you stood there stripped of your garments before the crowd. Yet, you endured that humiliation for love of us. *(Kneel)* |
| **All** | Lord Jesus, I may face in my life persons who want to strip me of my self-esteem or my sense of integrity. I may face individuals who ridicule me, reject me, or snub me because of my Christian conviction and belief in your Gospel message.

As I face such humiliation and insult, may I think of you standing on Calvary stripped of your garments. May I speak no evil against others nor retaliate with hatred, but respond as you would. May I know how to forgive from the heart and show compassion for those who have wronged me. May I continue to forgive others, as others have forgiven me for the wrongs I have done. |
Leader	Lord Jesus crucified,
All	Have mercy on me a sinner. *(Stand)*
	Hymn

The Eleventh Station | JESUS IS NAILED TO THE CROSS

Leader	We adore you, O Christ, and we praise you. ***(Kneel)***
All	For by your holy cross you have redeemed the world. ***(Stand)***
Leader	What excruciating pain you must have experienced, Lord Jesus, as the soldiers drove the nails into your wrists and feet! Yet you bore this pain willingly as an expression of your deep love for us. ***(Kneel)***
All	Lord Jesus, in the spirit of Christian love, help me to deal with the pain I face in life. Help me to reach out to others to forgive them, to bring them your healing grace, to go out of my way for them. With love, all things are possible, even in the midst of pain, sorrow and discomfort. Lord Jesus, strengthen me in my love for you; strengthen me in my love for others.
Leader	Lord Jesus crucified,
All	Have mercy on me a sinner. ***(Stand)***
	Hymn

The Twelfth Station | JESUS DIES ON THE CROSS

Leader	We adore you, O Christ, and we praise you. *(Kneel)*
All	For by your holy cross you have redeemed the world. *(Stand)*
Leader	The moment finally came, Jesus, when you breathed your last on the tree of the cross. The tree of the garden of Paradise yields now to the tree of life on which you, the new Adam, died. You willingly gave your life as part of your Father's plan. In that great act of obedience and love, you have given us the gift of new life, and ushered us into the presence of your Father. Your great suffering shows the depths of your love for us! *(Kneel)*
All	May I learn from you, Lord Jesus, the true spirit of abandonment to the Father's will at all times, especially when that will seems so hard to understand. May my will be one with the will of your Father. Make me your faithful disciple as I die daily to self in order to bring life to others.
Leader	Lord Jesus crucified,
All	Have mercy on me a sinner. *(Stand)*
	Hymn

The Thirteenth Station
JESUS IS TAKEN DOWN FROM THE CROSS

Leader	We adore you, O Christ, and we praise you. *(Kneel)*
All	For by your holy cross you have redeemed the world. *(Stand)*
Leader	Lord Jesus, the total gift of yourself to the Father is now complete. Your body was gently removed from the cross and placed in the arms of your sorrowful Mother. What pain she must have felt as she held in her arms the now lifeless body of her only son—the body she had conceived and given birth to, the body she had nourished and cherished! *(Kneel)*
All	When I face the death of loved ones, Lord Jesus, may our Blessed Lady, our sorrowful Mother, be with me to help me face the pain of that loss. In those moments of mourning and sorrow, may I also share your gifts of kindness, thoughtfulness and concern for others who grieve.
Leader	Lord Jesus crucified,
All	Have mercy on me a sinner. *(Stand)*
	Hymn

The Fourteenth Station | JESUS IS PLACED IN THE TOMB

Leader	We adore you, O Christ, and we praise you. ***(Kneel)***
All	For by your holy cross you have redeemed the world. ***(Stand)***
Leader	Your journey of life has now ended, Lord Jesus. Your body was reverently placed in the tomb to await the day of resurrection. ***(Kneel)***
All	When I face the reality of death in my life, Jesus, may I know that others will remember me and pray for me, as they reverently place my lifeless body in the tomb. May I cherish all those who love me in life and at the moment of death.
Leader	Lord Jesus crucified,
All	Have mercy on me a sinner. ***(Stand)***
	Hymn

| The Fifteenth Station | THE RESURRECTION OF JESUS |

Leader	We adore you, O Christ, and we praise you. *(Kneel)*
All	For by your holy cross you have redeemed the world. *(Stand)*
Leader	Listen, Lord Jesus, again and again as we pray as a faith community: "Dying, you destroyed our death; rising, you restored our life; Lord Jesus, come in glory!"

    The power of your resurrection continues to touch our lives, as we face the reality of our daily dying to self in order to rise with you to new life. You live now in the power and mystery of your Church and your sacraments. *(Kneel)* |
| **All** | Risen Lord Jesus, may I sense your continued presence among us in your Church and in the power and mystery of your sacraments. May I sense your powerful presence in your holy Word and in the great gift you give us in the Holy Eucharist!

    May I truly witness to the power and presence of the risen Lord Jesus at work in the world today.

    Led by the grace of your Spirit, I go forth to proclaim your Good News to all! |
Leader	Lord Jesus crucified,
All	Have mercy on me a sinner. *(Stand)*
	Hymn

	(Prayer for the Intentions of Our Holy Father)
Leader	Let us proclaim the mystery of our faith:
All	Christ has died, Christ has risen, Christ will come again!
	Concluding Hymn
	(Following the concluding hymn, instrumental music may be played, as all present venerate the cross or a relic of the true cross.)

After each station, an appropriate hymn could be sung. The text of the *Stabat Mater* is included here for those who would like to use it. This poem by an unknown author dates from the 13th century and is used in the liturgy on the feast of Our Lady of Sorrows.

THE STABAT MATER

1. At the cross her station keeping,
   Stood the mournful Mother weeping,
   Close to Jesus to the last.

2. Through her heart, his sorrow sharing,
   All his bitter anguish bearing,
   Now at length the sword had passed.

3. O how sad and sore distressed
   Was that Mother highly blest
   Of the sole-begotten one!

4. Christ above in torment hangs;
   She beneath beholds the pangs
   Of her dying glorious Son.

5. Is there one who would not weep,
   Whelmed in miseries so deep
   Christ's dear Mother to behold?

6. Can the human heart refrain
   From partaking in her pain,
   In that Mother's pain untold?

7. Bruised, derided, cursed, defiled,
   She beheld her tender Child
   All with bloody scourges rent.

8. For the sins of his own nation
   She saw him hang in desolation,
   Till his spirit forth he sent.

9. O my Mother, fount of love,
   Touch my spirit from above;
   Make my heart with yours accord.

10. Make me feel as you have felt;
    Make my soul to glow and melt
    With the love of Christ my Lord.

11. Holy Mother, pierce me through;
    In my heart each wound renew
    Of my Savior crucified.

12. Let me share with you his pain,
    Who for all my sins was slain,
    Who for me in torment died.

13. Let me mingle tears with you,
    Mourning him who mourned for me,
    All the days that I may live.

14. By the cross with you to stay,
    There with you to weep and pray,
    Is all I ask of you to give.

15. Christ, when you shall call me hence
    Be your Mother my defense;
    Be your cross my victory.

ABOUT THE AUTHOR

A priest for twenty-seven years and a bishop for eight years, Bishop Grosz serves as an auxiliary for the diocese of Buffalo, NY. He is also the pastor of Holy Trinity and St. Stanislaus Kostka Churches in Niagara Falls, NY.

Pauline BOOKS & MEDIA

The Daughters of St. Paul operate book and media centers at the following addresses. Visit, call or write the one nearest you today, or find us on the World Wide Web, www.pauline.org

CALIFORNIA
3908 Sepulveda Blvd, Culver City, CA 90230   310-397-8676
5945 Balboa Avenue, San Diego, CA 92111   858-565-9181
46 Geary Street, San Francisco, CA 94108   415-781-5180

FLORIDA
145 S.W. 107th Avenue, Miami, FL 33174   305-559-6715

HAWAII
1143 Bishop Street, Honolulu, HI 96813   808-521-2731
Neighbor Islands call: 800-259-8463

ILLINOIS
172 North Michigan Avenue, Chicago, IL 60601
312-346-4228

LOUISIANA
4403 Veterans Memorial Blvd, Metairie, LA 70006
504-887-7631

MASSACHUSETTS
885 Providence Hwy, Dedham, MA 02026   781-326-5385

MISSOURI
9804 Watson Road, St. Louis, MO 63126   314-965-3512

NEW JERSEY
561 U.S. Route 1, Wick Plaza, Edison, NJ 08817   732-572-1200

NEW YORK
150 East 52nd Street, New York, NY 10022   212-754-1110
78 Fort Place, Staten Island, NY 10301   718-447-5071

PENNSYLVANIA
9171-A Roosevelt Blvd, Philadelphia, PA 19114   215-676-9494

SOUTH CAROLINA
243 King Street, Charleston, SC 29401   843-577-0175

TENNESSEE
4811 Poplar Avenue, Memphis, TN 38117   901-761-2987

TEXAS
114 Main Plaza, San Antonio, TX 78205   210-224-8101

VIRGINIA
1025 King Street, Alexandria, VA 22314   703-549-3806

CANADA
3022 Dufferin Street, Toronto, Ontario, Canada M6B 3T5   416-781-9131
1155 Yonge Street, Toronto, Ontario, Canada M4T 1W2   416-934-3440

¡También somos su fuente para libros, videos y música en español!